# the cards of tl

CW01645985

## the major arcana

0. The Fool
1. The Magician
2. The High Priestess
3. The Empress
4. The Emperor
5. The Hierophant
6. The Lovers
7. The Chariot
8. Strength
9. The Hermit
10. Wheel of Fortune
11. Justice
12. The Hanged Man
13. Death
14. Temperance
15. The Devil
16. The Tower
17. The Star
18. The Moon
19. The Sun
20. Judgment
21. The World

# the cards of the tarot

## the suit of wands

22. Ace of Wands
23. Two of Wands
24. Three of Wands
25. Four of Wands
26. Five of Wands
27. Six of Wands
28. Seven of Wands
29. Eight of Wands
30. Nine of Wands
31. Ten of Wands
32. Page of Wands
33. Knight of Wands
34. Queen of Wands
35. King of Wands

# the cards of the tarot

## the suit of cups

36. Ace of Cups
37. Two of Cups
38. Three of Cups
39. Four of Cups
40. Five of Cups
41. Six of Cups
42. Seven of Cups
43. Eight of Cups
44. Nine of Cups
45. Ten of Cups
46. Page of Cups
47. Knight of Cups
48. Queen of Cups
49. King of Cups

# the cards of the tarot

## the suit of swords

50. Ace of Swords
51. Two of Swords
52. Three of Swords
53. Four of Swords
54. Five of Swords
55. Six of Swords
56. Seven of Swords
57. Eight of Swords
58. Nine of Swords
59. Ten of Swords
60. Page of Swords
61. Knight of Swords
62. Queen of Swords
63. King of Swords

# the cards of the tarot

## the suit of pentacles

64. Ace of Pentacles
65. Two of Pentacles
66. Three of Pentacles
67. Four of Pentacles
68. Five of Pentacles
69. Six of Pentacles
70. Seven of Pentacles
71. Eight of Pentacles
72. Nine of Pentacles
73. Ten of Pentacles
74. Page of Pentacles
75. Knight of Pentacles
76. Queen of Pentacles
77. King of Pentacles

# how to read tarot cards

When you are reading tarot cards for the first time, the best practice is to first take some time to meditate with your cards, and shuffle them while doing so. This will help you and your deck become familiar with each other.

Some people choose to cleanse their deck by placing special crystals on top of it, or to cleanse it by waving incense on top of the deck, or on each card of the deck. Some readers also just place their deck in sunlight for a few hours, or in a window during the full moon.

None of these methods are strictly necessary, but may help you feel more attached to your first tarot deck.

When you are ready, shuffle your cards, meditate on the question you wish to ask, and pick a card to place face down on a flat surface for each question. In the next pages, I will detail ways to lay out your cards to best answer your questions.

# how to read tarot cards

Many tarot readers do a "getting to know you", or "interview" spread with their new decks, which might look something like this:

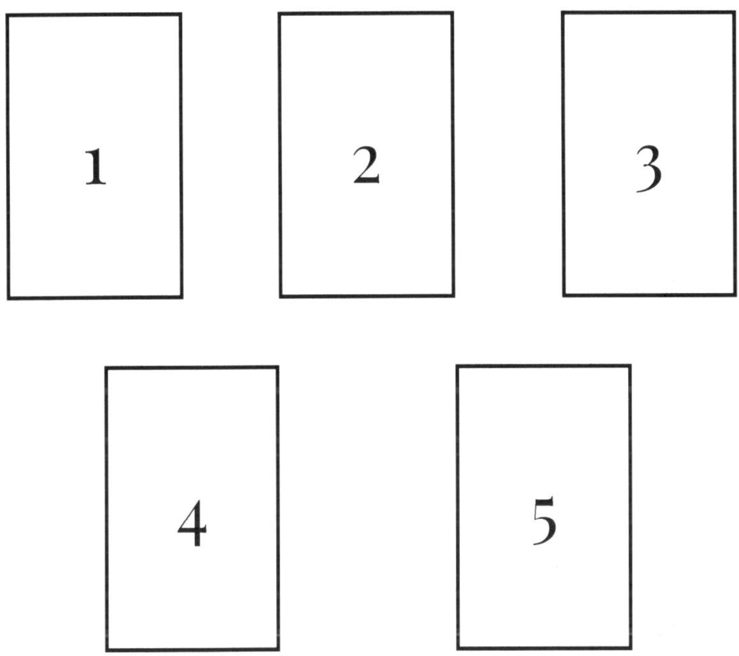


Where the meaning of the cards are as follows:

1.What are the strengths of this deck?
2. What kind of questions is this deck best for?
3. How can I best work with this deck?
4. What can you teach me?
5. What does this deck want from me?

# how to read tarot cards

Once you are familiar with your deck, another good spread is a classic 3 card spread, which can be used for a wide range of questions.

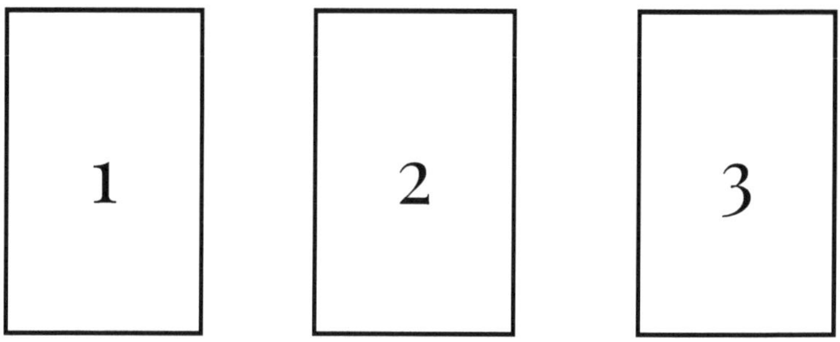


Some of the ways you could use this spread include:

1. Past
2. Present
3. Future

1. You
2. Your path
3. The potential future

1. You
2. The relationship
3. The other party (a partner, friend, etc)

# how to read tarot cards

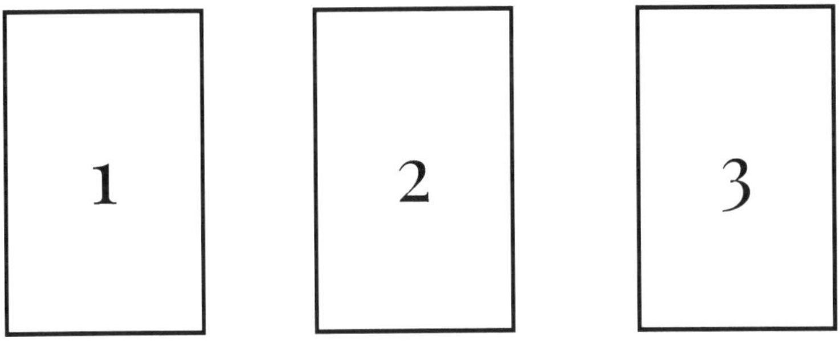


More 3 card spreads include:

1. The situation
2. The action you need to take
3. What the outcome will be

You can use it to weigh up different options:

1. The outcome of option 1
2. The outcome of option 2
3. The outcome of option 3

1. The situation
2. The obstacle you face
3. Advice for facing the obstacle

Alternatively, you can just ask the deck a question - and using this spread and the definitions within this book, combine the information together to reach your answer.

# how to use this book:

Now that you know how to create a tarot spread, you can shuffle & select your cards. Once you have done so, flip over your cards, and locate them within this book.

On the previous pages are a list of each of the tarot cards, in order of how they are presented in this book (and in the traditional order). You can use this to locate where in the book your card is located.

In each section, there will be a brief overview of that suit. After that, each tarot card will be featured on its own page, with key words indicating the meaning of the card when it is both upright, and reversed (meaning upside down).

Use these key words to guide you - not every card will mean the same exact thing for every person. Meditate on these meanings, and find which resonate the most with you. With time, you will find that certain definitions and meanings apply more to you than others.

# how to use this book:

In this book, I have used images of the Rider Waite tarot, originally published in 1909 and now within the public domain. It is the most well known and widely used of the tarot decks, as it has clear and evocative imagery for each of the cards, which will also be a great help to you in interpreting their meaning. However, your own deck may look different.

If you ever struggle to relate to any of the meanings I have provided, I'd suggest taking some time to look at the imagery on the card - both on your deck (if it's different), and on the Rider Waite deck. There may be features that jump out to you, or imagery that means something special to you.

# regarding upright and reversed cards

Some tarot readers choose not to read cards that appear reversed (upside down) any differently from upright cards, and choose to use the upright interpretation for each card. Some people choose not to read these are their interpretations can sometimes be more negative, or are simply more cards to memorise. It is a personal choice, and I would recommend you pick what seems the most appealing to you.

It is my personal recommendation that you begin with only upright cards for your first few tarot spreads, and then start using reversals. If you find they don't resonate with you after several spreads, I would stick to reading upright cards only.

# the major arcana

the major arcana represent the biggest things in life - major decisions, life lessons, and the big meanings impacting your life.

major arcana cards typically indicate big, life changing events.

0

# the fool

## upright

new beginnings • innocence • naivety • idealism • undertaking a new adventure

## reversed

recklessness • not ready to take the next step • fear of the unknown • holding back

1

# the magician

## upright

manifesting • you can make your own dreams come true • create your vision • be focused • willpower

## reversed

uncertainty • follow your intuition • lack of progress • being tricked or manipulated • be wary of greed

2

# the high priestess

## upright

a strong sense of intuition • trust your inner voice • femininity • powerful women • subconscious knowledge

## reversed

not trusting your own intuition • repression of emotion • secrets • lying and untruths

3

# the empress

## upright

femininity • fertility • beauty • abundance • nature • new projects, ideas • the archetypal mother

## reversed

over-reliance on others • smothering others & being smothered • lack of independence and self-confidence

4

# the emperor

## upright

authority • structure • stability • control • be practical • discipline • father figure

## reversed

dominance • someone controlling • stubbornness • rigidity & inflexibility • power dynamics

5

# the hierophant

## upright

spiritual wisdom • religion • tradition • institutions • conformity • morality and ethics

## reversed

rebellion from tradition • subversiveness • challenging the status quo • freedom

6

# the lovers

## upright

love • marriage • romantic unions • coming together • aligning values • making choices

## reversed

self love • disharmony • romantic imbalance • misaligned values • conflict • bad choices • indecision

7

# the chariot

## upright

travel • moving • success • willpower • vehicles & transportation • ambition • determination

## reversed

lack of direction • feeling stuck • obstacles • frustration & aggression • obstacles

8

# strength

## upright

inner strength • courage • focus • passion • focus • loving, calm energy • "taming the beast"

## reversed

lack of courage • weakness • self doubt • insecurity • untamed emotions

9

# the hermit

## upright

taking time away from the world • peaceful solitude • self reflection • introspection • soul searching

## reversed

loneliness • isolation • rejection • withdrawal • returning to society

10

# the wheel of fortune

## upright

good luck • life cycles • destiny & fate • big, positive changes • unexpected events • decisive moments

## reversed

bad luck • resisting necessary change • unwelcome changes • breaking negative cycles

# justice

## upright

justice & fairness • the law • truth & honesty • cause & effect • integrity • accountability

## reversed

injustice • retribution • lack of accountability • dishonesty • corruption

12

# the hanged man

## upright

uncertainty • contemplation • lack of direction • different perspectives • waiting, pausing • surrending

## reversed

stalling • stagnating • avoiding necessary sacrifice • apathy • coming to a standstill

13

# death

## upright

not literal death • change • transformation • transition • endings & beginnings • letting go

## reversed

resisting change • being stuck in negative patterns • stagnation

14

# temperance

## upright

balance • moderation • purpose • patience • calm & tranquility • serenity

## reversed

imbalance • excess • extremes • self healing must be done to move forward

15

# the devil

## upright

obsessed • dependency • addiction • excess • powerlessness • shadow self

## reversed

reclaiming power & control • releasing limiting beliefs • exploring and challenging dark thoughts

16

# the tower

## upright

big, extreme changes • upheaval • chaos • sudden change • revelation • self awakening

## reversed

avoiding disaster • fear of change • personal transformation

17

# the star

## upright

hope • faith • wishes • positivity & optimism • healing • self renewal • purpose

## reversed

lack of faith & hope • despair • negativity • overwhelmed by obstacles • learn to trust the universe

18

# the moon

## upright

anxiety & fear • intuition • subconscious thoughts • illusions • secrets • complexity • confusion

## reversed

fear • deception • lack of clarity • a need to let go of fear • repressed emotion • confusion

# the sun

## upright

positivity, warmth, optimism • good omens • success • radiant joy • enthusiasm • self confidence

## reversed

happiness is possible, but blocked • negativity • inner child work • need for direction

20

# judgment

## upright

internal awakening • reflection • rebirth • inner callings • reckoning • revelations

## reversed

lack of self awareness • not learning life lessons • low self esteem & self criticism • ignoring your calling

21

# the world

## upright

the completion of a journey • an achievement • travel • feelings of wholeness • feelings of belonging

## reversed

a need for closure • delays, particularly to travel • feeling a lack of achievement

# the suit of wands

the suit of wands represent energy, spirituality, creativity & inspiration, art, and artistic expression.

the suit of wands is associated with the element of fire.

they are associated with the fire signs: aries, leo, and sagittarius.

the kinds of people that are often associated with wands are energetic, chaotic, warm, and spiritual.

# ace of wands

## upright

new project • inspiration • creativity • you have the potential for incredible growth • surmountable challenges

## reversed

the beginning of an idea • lack of direction • false starts • delays • rejection • distractions

# two of wands

## upright

planning for the future • progress • waiting for an answer • decision making • choices • travel •

## reversed

lack of planning • travel delays • not seeing the bigger picture, thinking too small • fear of the unknown

# three of wands

## upright

carefully planning for the future • progress • expansion • foresight • travel, particularly overseas •

## reversed

a lack of planning causing problems • delays • setbacks • not seeing the bigger picture

25

# four of wands

## upright

celebrations • happiness • joy • harmony • reunions • closeness and celebrating with family and friends

## reversed

moving • conflict with others• leaving a family unit • personal celebrations • inner harmony • transitions

26

# five of wands

## upright

rivalry • conflicts • tension • obstacles • diversity • meaningless conflict • inability to find common ground

## reversed

conflict avoidance • inner conflict • release of tension

# six of wands

## upright

victory, success • good news is coming • public recognition of your achievements • self confidence

## reversed

isolation after failure • a lack of confidence leads to giving up • private achievements • redefining success

28

# seven of wands

## upright

challenge • competition • perseverance • lack of clarity • protecting what is yours

## reversed

not having strong enough boundaries • quitting • exhaustion • overwhelm

# eight of wands

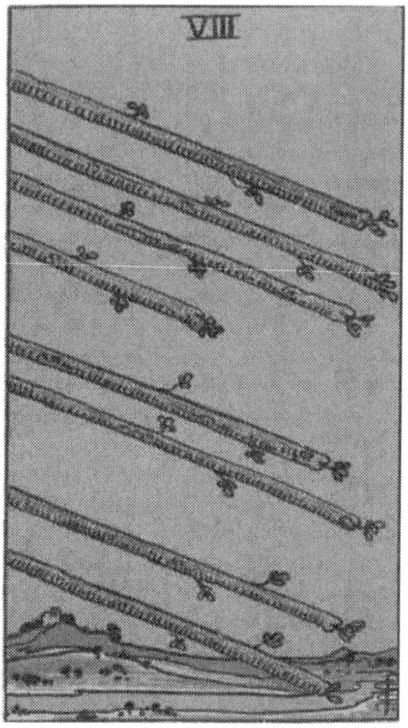

## upright

big news • fast paced changes • action • travel, particularly by air • movement

## reversed

frustrations • delays, particularly to travel • problems ahead • resisting necessary change

# nine of wands

## upright

persistence & tenaciousness • keep your boundaries strong • have courage • near the finish line

## reversed

do not isolate yourself • have faith in yourself and others • defensiveness • use your inner resources

# ten of wands

## upright

stress • exhaustion & burnout • too many responsibilities & burdens • hard work

## reversed

taking a break • time to relax • saying no • trying to do it all • release

32

# page of wands

## upright

a new project or creative outlet • limitless potential • free spirit • inspiration • discovery • new ideas

## reversed

immaturity • newly formed ideas • self-limiting beliefs • redirecting your energy

33

# knight of wands

## upright

a free-spirited person • romance and flirtatiousness • energy • passion • impulsiveness

## reversed

a chaotic person • impulsivity • lack of romantic commitment • passion project • scattered energy

34

# queen of wands

## upright

charm • courage • confidence • determination • social activities, or a social person • independence

## reversed

self respect • self confidence • shyness and introversion • a lack of self knowledge

# king of wands

## upright

a natural leader • a strong vision • entrepreneurship • awards and honours • life and creativity • strength

## reversed

impulsiveness • ruthlessness • high expectations • harshness

# the suit of cups

the cups represent emotion, feeling, and consciousness. they are associated with love, connections, and friendships. you will often see them in readings about romance, communication & friendships.

the suit of cups is associated with the element of water, and the star signs of cancer, pisces, and scorpio.

the kinds of people that are personified by the suit of cups are emotional, introspective, expressive, emotionally intelligent, and think with their hearts over their heads.

# ace of cups

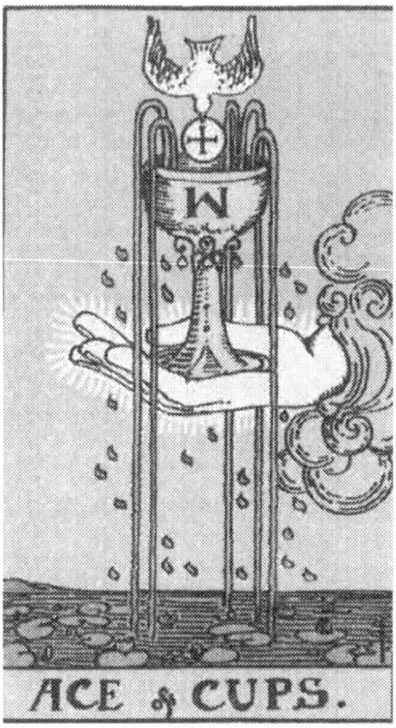


## upright

new love • a new baby, relationship, or marriage • compassion • creativity • divine love • conscious awareness

## reversed

a need for self love • emotional repression • love yourself first • intuition

# two of cups

## upright

romantic love • partnerships • proposals • marriage • unions • mutual attraction • passionate energy

## reversed

breakups • separations • arguments • disinterest • self love • distrust • a rocky relationship

# three of cups

## upright

friendships • celebrations • a strong support system • collaboration with others

## reversed

gossiping about others • excessive partying • a lack of support • a third wheel • alone time

# four of cups

## upright

apathy • lack of fulfilment • meditation & contemplation • time to reevaluate

## reversed

a new outlook • new doors opening • realigning yourself to your goals and ideals

# five of cups

## upright

loss • grief • regrets • don't be so focused on your failures that you can't move forward • pessimism • failure

## reversed

moving on • forgiveness • hope • recovery • accepting personal setbacks

41

# six of cups

## upright

fond memories of the past • memories • childhood nostalgia • gifts • innocence • reunions • innocence

## reversed

living in the past • naivety • unrealistic expectations for those around you • lacking playfulness

# seven of cups

## upright

too many options • commitment issues • be careful of what you wish for, not everything is as it seems

## reversed

clarity • restored sense of judgment • illusions are revealed • too many choices

43

# eight of cups

## upright

moving on • withdrawing from negative situations • abandonment • escapism • difficult journeys ahead

## reversed

learning from your past • returning home • trying one more time • indecisiveness • walking away

# nine of cups

## upright

wishes coming true • abundance • good health • joy • satisfaction • gratitude

## reversed

greed or materialism • physical ill health • be wary of quick results • indulgence

# ten of cups

## upright

family • contentment & happiness • total love and support • harmony • perfect alignment • domestic bliss

## reversed

family trouble • relationship issues • empty nest • disconnection • values are not aligned

# page of cups

## upright

new love • volunteer work • new creative opportunities • pay attention to your intuition • be curious

## reversed

doubting your intuition • immaturity • breakups • fear is getting in the way of your journey

# knight of cups

## upright

someone that embodies your dream romantic partner • romance • proposals • beauty • imagination

## reversed

a brooding or moody individual • unrealistic expectations • an overactive imagination • jealousy

# queen of cups

## upright

a nurturing, supportive person • healing • support • compassion • intuition • introspection

## reversed

feeling smothered, or smothering others • insecurity • codependence • focus on self care and self love

49

# king of cups

## upright

a supportive leader or boss • empathy • tolerance • emotional balance • diplomacy

## reversed

emotional manipulation • brooding or moodiness • focus on self compassion • listen to your inner feelings

# the suit of swords

the suit of swords represent thought, intellect, intelligence, our minds and beliefs. you will see them present often in relation to knowledge, action, and change.

swords are associated with the element of air, and the air signs of gemini, libra, and aquarius.

the kinds of people that are personified by the suit of swords are clever, quick witted, powerful, and action oriented.

# ace of swords

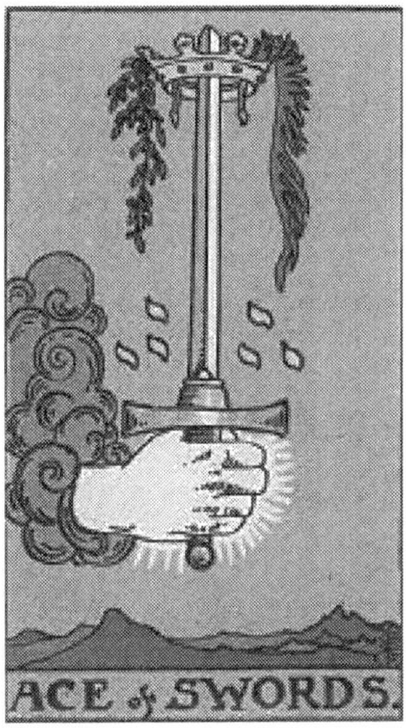


## upright

breakthrough ideas • mental clarity • new ideas • intellectual success • triumph • be prepared for challenges

## reversed

stress • mental blocks • lack of inner clarity • poor judgment • deceit & dishonesty • rethinking ideas

# two of swords

## upright

compromise • decision making • difficult choices • missing relevant information • weighing options

## reversed

confusion • indecision • overwhelm • compromise • a stalemate • feeling stuck • get more information

# three of swords

## upright

heartbreak • divorce & breakups • loss • depression • sorrow • emotional pain

## reversed

apologising & forgiveness • healing • reduce negative self talk • release your pain

# four of swords

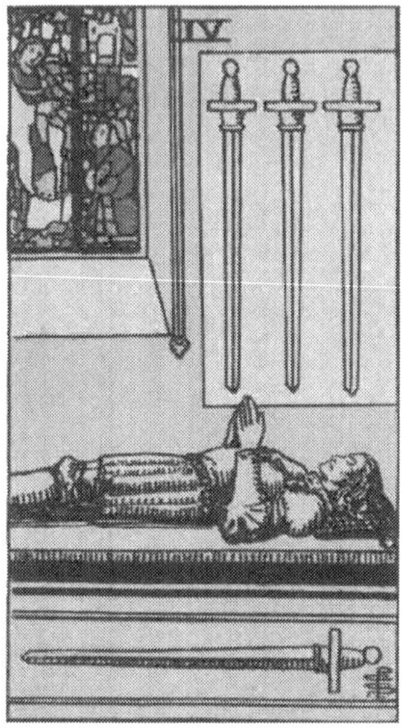


## upright

rest • solitude • recovery • take time to recuperate and contemplate your next steps forward • singular focus

## reversed

restlessness • anxiety • overwhelm • burnout • time for contemplation is needed • stagnation

54

# five of swords

## upright

unhealthy relationships • conflict & disagreements • seek the deeper meaning of conflict

## reversed

reconciliation • peace after conflict • seek to let go of past resentment • make amends

# six of swords

## upright

necessary change and transition • relocating • rite of passage • carrying baggage from the past • a peaceful future

## reversed

unfinished business • issues with travel or moving • resistance to change

56

# seven of swords

## upright

betrayal • dishonesty • running away from a situation • you need to be strategic about your next steps

## reversed

impostor syndrome • trust that you have everything you already need to succeed

57

# eight of swords

## upright

self-imposed restrictions • isolation • negative thoughts • learned helplessness

## reversed

self criticism • releasing negative thoughts • seek and be open to new perspectives

# nine of swords

## upright

anxiety, worry, fear • nightmares • depression • your worry is creating a self fulfilling prophecy • seek support

## reversed

deep seated fears • inner turmoil • recovery • relief from past difficult situations

# ten of swords

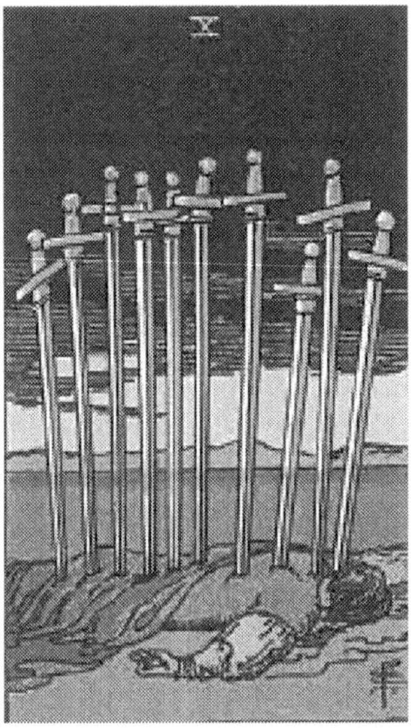

## upright

a complete or painful ending • rock bottom • crisis • the end of a drawn out and painful situation

## reversed

a new start • recovery • forgiveness • moving on • do not resist the inevitable change

# page of swords

## upright

new ideas • intellectual curiosity • communication • ideas that create positive change • sharing ideas

## reversed

holding back from expressing yourself • be wary of acting impulsively or hastily • think your actions through

# knight of swords

## upright

ambition • action • fast thinking • a lifestyle change • diving headfirst into a situation or project • assertiveness

## reversed

inability to channel your energy productively • lack of focus • slow down to gain focus

# queen of swords

## upright

someone self-sufficient and independent • honesty & unbiased judgement • direct communication

## reversed

a cold, unemotional person • rigid logic • dishonesty • unkindness

# king of swords

## upright

an intentional & natural leader • strategy • a clear head • a powerful intellect • authority

## reversed

corruption or misuse of power • seek your inner truth • learning to be more powerful within yourself

# the suit of pentacles

the suit of pentacles represent our physical worlds - money, career, and material goods. they will most often appear in readings about finances and careers, though they can often appear in relation to our self-esteem, self-image, and our ego.

the suit of pentacles is associated with the element of earth, and the earth signs of capricorn, virgo, and taurus.

the kind of person that is personified by the suit of pentacles is grounded, practical, tactile, stable, and strong.

# ace of pentacles

## upright

a new job • a promotion or raise • investments • new income • positive financial and material change

## reversed

worrying about money • going into debt • losing an opportunity • a need for planning & foresight

# two of pentacles

## upright

weighing up two choices • multi-tasking • decision making • manage your time efficiently

## reversed

inability to commit, or being over-committed • overwhelm • a need to re-prioritise your life

# three of pentacles

## upright

collaboration • a skilled team coming together • sharing knowledge • you have everything you need to succeed

## reversed

office politics • a lack of support from others • misalignment between individuals • solitary work

# four of pentacles

## upright

over-attachment to finances • a mindset of scarcity • fear of poverty • don't lose sight of what truly matters

## reversed

poverty • fear of poverty • vulnerability • overspending • a desire for stability

# five of pentacles

## upright

worry • isolation • financial loss • lack mindset • don't be so focused on your worries you miss opportunities

## reversed

a new job • a new home • hope • recovery • now is the time to focus on spiritual growth

# six of pentacles

## upright

giving or receiving help • generosity & kindness • fairness • be generous with your resources when you can

## reversed

one-sided charity • unpaid debts • a need to take time for self care • don't give to others at your own expense

# seven of pentacles

## upright

patience • receiving the rewards of your hard work after waiting • delayed success • investments

## reversed

giving up too soon • work with no reward • a lack of long-term planning or visions

# eight of pentacles

## upright

skill mastery • loving your job • apprenticeships or training • learning new skills • hard work creates success

## reversed

lack of focus and ambition • perfectionism • self development • focusing on the wrong area

# nine of pentacles

## upright

self-sufficient • financial gain • individual hobbies • material luxury and abundance • beauty

## reversed

don't overwork yourself • jealousy • envy • financial setbacks • know that you deserve as much as others

# ten of pentacles

## upright

your legacy & lineage • retirement • inheritance • passing on the torch • financial security • long term success

## reversed

family conflicts • loneliness • feelings of failure or loss • question what you do because it is expected of you

# page of pentacles

## upright

a new job • a raise • money news • manifestation • growing new skills • manifesting abundance

## reversed

problems with learning or studying • feeling as though you are not progressing • learn from your failure

75

# knight of pentacles

## upright

someone reliable and hardworking • patience • hard work • routine • traditions

## reversed

a stubborn individual • laziness • feeling stuck • a need to cultivate self discipline

# queen of pentacles

## upright

resourcefulness • fertility & pregnancy • domestic life • domestic bliss • working parents • nurturing

## reversed

self care is needed • conflict between work and home lives • seeking financial independence

77

# king of pentacles

## upright

a practical person • wisdom • sound financial investments • business advice • material abundance

## reversed

lack of follow through • jealousy • an excessive focus on wealth and status • stubbornness

Printed in Great Britain
by Amazon

32370063R00053